GHOSTS

Every year, around the world, there are hundreds of sightings of the mysterious things people call ghosts. Despite the advances made by modern science, ghosts have not been explained. Some say that they are just hallucinations, others that they are as real as the people who see them. In the following pages are described some accounts of the most exciting, interesting and terrifying ghostly experiences. Read about an entire battle fought by ghosts, the ghost of a fighter pilot who came back to clear his name and poltergeists that make houses go bump in the night. Consider the evidence put forward and see if you can get to the bottom of some of the strangest ghostly mysteries.

GREAT MYSTERIES

MYSTERIES

GHOSTS

Rupert Matthews

Illustrated by Michael Bragg

Wayland

Great Mysteries

Ancient Mysteries
Ghosts
Lands of Legend
Lost Treasure
Monster Mysteries
Sea Mysteries
The Supernatural
UFOs

Editor : William Wharfe
Designer: David Armitage
Cover Illustration: The ghost of the beheaded Anne Boleyn, who was once wife of King Henry VIII, drives out into the night, away from her former home of Blickling Hall.

Frontispiece: On 11 June 1881, Prince George, later King George V, along with others on HMS *Inconstant* saw what may have been the ghost-ship *Flying Dutchman*.

First Published in 1989 by
Wayland (Publishers) Limited
61 Western Road, Hove
East Sussex BN3 1JD

British Library Cataloguing-In-Publication Data
Matthews, Rupert
   Ghosts. – (Great Mysteries)
   1. Ghosts
   I. Title II. Series
   133.1

ISBN 1–85210–641–7

Typeset by Lizzie George, Wayland
Printed in Italy by G. Canale & C.S.p.A., Turin
Bound in the UK at The Bath Press, Avon

Contents

Introduction: what is a ghost?

Above *Ghosts are popular subjects for movies. The 1988 release* Betelgeuse *featured a crazy spirit of that name.*

Below *This photograph was taken in Lincoln Cathedral. Nobody else was present at the time, so who is the figure on the right? Is it a ghost?*

Most people are familiar with ghost films and books. In such tales phantom monks flit through the night and figures wrapped in sheets chase frightened people from their homes. In horror films, supernatural forces may be unleashed in all sorts of terrifying forms.

Such tales make exciting drama, but they are very rarely true stories. However, evidence from some carefully-recorded incidents suggests that ghosts may in fact be real. Some ghosts that have been reported are every bit as terrifying as those in films and books.

A ghost or phantom is generally thought of as the image of a dead person that appears to humans. However, some ghosts are of things or animals rather than of people. Different ghosts behave in different ways, just as living people do. A few spectres are frightening, or even dangerous, but most are perfectly harmless. The only damage they do is to shock the people who see them.

The one thing that all ghosts have in common is that they appear to come from nowhere and then vanish into thin air. Except for the time they are seen or heard, it is as if they do not exist. It is this that causes many people to believe that ghosts do not exist. According to the laws of science it is impossible for an object to vanish without trace or to be formed out of nothing. It is therefore suggested that 'ghosts' are just cases of mistaken identification. In one recent report by a university team, more than 300 'ghost reports' were studied. The scientists concluded that all these apparitions were hallucinations, but offered no evidence to support this conclusion.

This book looks at some of the different types of ghost that have been reported. Evidence for these phantoms is presented, together with possible explanations for what occurs. Readers will have to decide for themselves if they believe that ghosts really exist and, if they do, what they are.

Above *This famous photograph was taken by Arthur Springer, a retired policeman, in 1916. The headless dog was not visible to anyone at the time the picture was taken.*

Cavalry charge to nowhere

On a summer's day in 1863 John and Henry, two farmers who live near the town of Shiloh on the banks of the Tennessee River are walking home for lunch. It is a bright, sunny day and the men are hot and thirsty.

Suddenly John cries out 'Look, there are some soldiers.' Henry turns to look in the direction his friend is pointing. He can see a group of about 100 soldiers running across a field. He is surprised because the main armies fighting the American Civil War are many kilometres away. He cannot imagine why so many soldiers are near Shiloh. The two men decide to run home to warn their families that the armies have returned to Shiloh, where a large battle had been fought in April 1862.

The men hurry along the road, but jump behind a tree at the side of the road when they see a troop of cavalry charging towards them with sabres raised and guns firing. Suddenly Henry notices that the horses are making no noise as they gallop. As the men watch, other soldiers come into sight, marching silently in a long column. Henry realizes that they are watching a ghostly re-enactment of the battle which took place more than a year before. The soldiers move in the same direction as they had done in the real battle. After a few minutes the phantoms vanish and the two men run home to tell everyone what they have seen.

Phantom replays

Above *The Tower of London, where the phantom of the Countess of Salisbury is said to re-enact her gruesome execution.*

Some of the most dramatic ghosts are those which seem to re-enact events from the past. Such phantoms appear from nowhere, perform certain actions and then vanish. Each time they are seen the ghosts behave in exactly the same way. They never react to living people nor to their surroundings. It is as if a three-dimensional video recording was being played.

On the night of 12 January 1913 a man was murdered beside a lamppost in Calle Jujuy, a street in Buenos Aires, Argentina. Several weeks later the ghost of the man was seen to walk along the street to the fatal lamppost, turn round in terror and then vanish. Many people claim to have witnessed the ghost retracing its final steps in life. Each time it is seen the ghost performs exactly the same actions.

A similar re-enactment of death is occasionally seen at the Tower of London. In 1541 the Countess of Salisbury, who was innocent of the crimes with which she was charged, was taken to the Tower to be executed. She was dragged screaming to the scaffold, but broke free from her guards and tried to escape. The executioner ran after her, swiping at her with his axe.

Right *Prince Rupert leads his dashing Cavaliers in an attack on the Parliamentarian army during the Battle of Edgehill. It was scenes such as this that were replayed by the phantom of Edgehill.*

After some minutes the countess was caught and beheaded on the spot. Several startled visitors and residents at the Tower have seen this terrible event played out by ghosts of the countess and her ruthless guards.

Not all victims of beheadings are seen at the site of their execution. Anne Boleyn, queen of Henry VIII and one of the most famous women to die on the scaffold, has been seen at her childhood home of Blickling Hall. Sometimes she is seen quietly strolling in the gardens. On other occasions Anne is seen as she was carried from the scaffold, with her head tucked underneath her arm.

Equally dramatic were the ghosts that terrified villagers in Warwickshire 300 years ago. In this case thousands of phantoms appeared at once. On 23 October 1643 a battle was fought at Edgehill between Cavaliers and Roundheads during the English Civil War. About a month after the battle two shepherds were amazed to see a second battle taking place on the same site. They fled, but found out later that no soldiers were close by.

On Christmas Eve, the ghostly soldiers returned to fight again. This time witnesses realized that they were watching a phantom replay of the battle of 23 October. When King Charles learnt of the ghosts, he sent a team of investigators to discover the truth. Not only did these men, led by Sir Lewis Kirk, interview witnesses, they even saw the phantom battle themselves. One of the team who had fought in the battle recognized many men who had died that day. More amazingly, he noticed the ghosts of men who had survived and still lived. After replaying itself several more times the battle vanished never to be seen again.

Above *The phantom Battle of Waterloo seen at Verviers.*

Perhaps the most well-known phantom replay involving a famous person is that which occurred in the White House – the official residence of the president of the USA. The ghost of the great president, Abraham Lincoln (president 1861-65) has been seen walking the corridors and watching what has been going on. The wife of President Franklin Roosevelt (who was in office 1933-45), Eleanor, was in her study working late one night when the maid, Mary Eban burst in, obviously terrified by something. She said, 'He's up there – sitting on the edge of the bed, taking off his boots!' When asked who 'He' was, Eban replied, 'Mr Lincoln!'

Not long after that, Mrs Roosevelt came across someone else with a similar experience. While Queen Wilhelmina of the Netherlands was staying at the White House, she was awakened one night by a knock at her bedroom door. She opened the door to find none other than Abraham Lincoln staring at her; she fainted with the shock of it! Some people think that President Lincoln's ghost was re-enacting one of the more traumatic moments of his stay in the White House.

Below *Some people, known as mediums, claim to be able to communicate with the spirits of people who have died. Here the Polish medium, Franek Kluski, is seen (second from the right) in 1925 with a figure which he claimed to be a spirit.*

Left *A portrait of the US President Abraham Lincoln, whose phantom is said to haunt his old home, the White House, in Washington DC.*

The type of ghost that simply recreates a scene from the past can be very disturbing for those who see them, but the phantoms take no notice of the living witness. They continue to repeat their actions time and again. This fact has led some investigators to suggest an explanation for these ghosts.

It has been observed that such replays are usually of dramatic and highly emotional events, often the moment of death. It is suggested that such strong emotions release some kind of force, often called psychic energy. This psychic energy may be absorbed by the surroundings and remain long after the event. It has been argued that some future event might trigger a release of this energy which emerges in the form of a phantom replay.

Evidence supporting this idea can be found in many reports of phantoms. It might be expected that psychic energy would fade over a period of years. Some ghosts do seem to be seen less clearly or less often as time passes. For instance one house was haunted in the eighteenth century by a woman dressed in red. In the nineteenth century witnesses said the phantom wore a pink dress. Some years later the ghost appeared in a white dress. By 1971 only a faint sound of footsteps remained. It seems that the clarity of the ghost faded with the years.

Below *Grace Rosher claimed to communicate with the dead by means of 'spirit writing', allowing the spirits to move her hand and so write messages.*

Warning from the water

It is a hot summer's day in 1921. Two Englishmen visiting the Hebrides decide to go for a stroll along the seashore. After walking for several kilometres the two men come across a beautiful little bay. Tumbled rocks surround the bay and shelter it from the ocean waves.

Harold decides to collect winkles for supper that night. He wades through the shallow water prising the shellfish from their rocks. James rests for a while, then changes to go for a swim. He climbs on to a rock and prepares to dive into the cool, smooth water.

Suddenly he cries out in terror. Rising out of the water is an apparition of a young woman. The figure floats in the air over the sea. She waves her arms, as if urging James not to enter the water. Faced with this phantom the two men flee the bay and return to their hotel.

They learn later that a young woman named Molly Machay drowned in the bay, some years earlier. Locals believe that her ghost appears whenever somebody swims in the bay, in the hope of preventing a second drowning.

Ghosts with a mission

A few ghosts seem to wander the earth and haunt the living for a particular purpose. They may appear just once, or several times. The style and persistence of these hauntings seems to depend on

Above *The fearsome phantom hound with glowing eyes, Black Shuck, which prowls the country lanes of England.*

The phantom hound

Country lanes of several parts of England are said to be haunted by a large black dog. Known by various names, such as Black Shuck or Striker, the hound is usually thought of as a demon. It is thought that the dog is an omen of bad luck to anyone who sees it.

the success, or failure, of the ghostly mission. As soon as the ghost achieves its aim, it vanishes never to be seen again. If, for some reason, the ghost fails to achieve what it wants, it may continue to appear for many years.

One of the best known phantoms with a mission appeared in Dubrach, a village in Scotland, in June 1750. It led to the uncovering of a baffling crime. The haunting began late at night when a farmer named Alexander MacPherson woke up to find a complete stranger in his bedroom. MacPherson's surprise turned to shock when the figure announced that it was the ghost of Sergeant Arthur Davies who had vanished a year earlier. The ghost said that Davies had been murdered. It then led MacPherson to a small hill where its earthly remains were hidden and demanded a proper burial. The phantom also named two men who, it claimed, were responsible for the murder. Then it vanished.

At first MacPherson was unsure what to do. He contacted a friend of Sergeant Davies' who recognized the clothes and personal objects on the corpse – they belonged to Davies. The body was then given a proper burial. Some time later the authorities heard about the discovery of the body. The men named by the ghost were then arrested and tried for murder. The judge, however, decided that the word of a ghost was not enough to hang the men, and allowed them to walk free. The ghost itself seems to have been satisfied with a decent burial and appeared no more.

More long lasting than the ghost of Sergeant Davies were the phantom Cavaliers of Hampton Court, Middlesex. These two spirits were seen many times from the seventeenth to the nineteenth centuries. They usually appeared in one particular section of the gardens. In 1871 maintenance work involved digging a trench near where the ghosts were seen. Two skeletons were found in a shallow grave. The bones were taken away and given a Christian burial. The ghosts never walked again.

Below *A courtyard at Hampton Court, Middlesex, which is said to be haunted by several ghosts, including that of Queen Catherine Howard and a mysterious procession of ladies.*

One of Australia's most famous ghosts was seen in broad daylight. In 1826, off the road between Sydney and Melbourne several people independently reported seeing a ghostly figure standing on a bridge pointing to a place in the creek below. Almost as soon as it was spotted, the figure would vanish. In fact, there were so many sightings that it was eventually decided by the authorities to investigate the area. When they started digging at the spot indicated by the ghost, they found the remains of Fred Fisher, who was a farmer and gold prospector. He had disappeared earlier that year.

The remains showed that Fisher had been murdered, and a search for the murderer was carried out. Finally, the culprit was found, tried and hanged. The ghost seems not to have appeared since, and the creek is now known as Fisher's Ghost Creek.

The mission of a phantom may not be entirely clear. On the Pacific islands of Fiji the ghost of a European woman, known as the White Lady, was reputed to haunt the town of Levuka. She was seen by many people, including a police officer. He became suspicious when he had seen her in several

Above A photograph taken in the Australian bush, which seems to show a ghostly figure. Nobody has ever proved this picture to be a fake.

Below The narrow bridge where several people claimed to have seen the ghost of Fisher.

places around the town and realized that she could not possibly have covered the distance from one place to another (in the time that she was out of sight) by any normal means. When the policeman went home that evening he opened the door to his house and there was the White Lady again! It was too much for him and he fainted.

Eventually the likeness of the ghost was matched with that of a German woman who died in Levuka early this century. Apparently her tomb had been badly damaged shortly before the sightings started. This fact connected with some of the signs people said they had seen the White Lady make.

The German woman's tomb was repaired. Since then, sightings of the White Lady have become much less frequent; her mission seems to have been fulfilled.

Ghosts that appear for a specific purpose are quite different from most ghosts. They seem to be aware of people and react to them – they are not simply recordings of past events.

Some people argue that this means that the ghosts are the spirits of the dead that continue to exist as phantoms. It is said that if something is worrying a person when they die, the soul may be somehow prevented from leaving until that matter is settled. In the cases of Sergeant Davies and the two Cavaliers, they may have realized that they would not be properly buried. This thought kept their spirits on earth until their burials were completed. This might indicate that the dead are aware of what happens to the living – how else would the spirits know that someone had gone to the trouble of burying their earthly remains properly?

Other investigations suggest different explanations. One of the most popular is the idea of suspended telepathy. This theory suggests that at the moment of death a person can send out a telepathic message. If this is not received at the time, it may continue to exist and be picked up in the form of a ghost. Once the message is received, the ghost disappears.

Above *The beautiful Pacific Island of Levuka, scene of a famous haunting earlier this century.*

Below *The photograph taken in 1936 which seems to show the 'Brown Lady of Raynham'. This ghost is said to have haunted the beautiful Raynham Hall in Norfolk for centuries.*

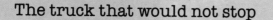

The truck that would not stop

It is a cold winter's evening and there has been a motor accident on the main road at Knightlow Hill, in England. Police Constable Forsythe trudges through the snow to reach the accident. He must clear the road and warn oncoming vehicles of the obstruction.

PC Forsythe arrives beside the crashed vehicles. Dusk is gathering so PC Forsythe and another man light a bonfire to alert drivers to the accident. It takes some time to set the damp wood alight, but at last a large blaze is started. A car approaches and slows down beside the fire. The driver asks PC Forsythe what is wrong.

The policeman is about to answer when another vehicle is heard approaching. It does not seem to be slowing down. A large truck is seen roaring along the road at high speed. PC Forsythe runs foward to signal the driver to halt, but he is ignored. The truck thunders past and heads straight for the crashed vehicles. PC Forsythe and the car driver stare in horror, expecting to witness a terrible collision. Suddenly the truck vanishes into thin air and PC Forsythe and the driver are left alone on the highway.

Phantom transport

Above *Once common, ghostly carriages seem to have become relatively rare in recent years.*

Among the most spectacular and mysterious phantoms are the ghostly vehicles, trains, ships and aeroplanes that are seen around the world. Most investigators explain ghosts as the souls of the dead or as recordings of highly emotional moments. However, machines have no soul and are incapable of feeling emotion. Whatever causes the spectral transports to appear must be a different kind of phenomenon.

One of the most famous of these ghosts is the *Flying Dutchman*. Stories concerning this phantom ship have been told for nearly three centuries. It is said that the ghost is that of a Dutch merchant ship captained by a man named Van der Decken. Trying to reach the East Indies, the ship ran into a terrible storm and Van der Decken cursed both God and the Devil in his anger. For this sin, it is said, Van der Decken is doomed to sail the seas for ever in his ancient ship.

Such a romantic tale could easily be dismissed as a legend were it not for the fact that many respectable people have reported sighting the *Flying Dutchman*. On the 11 June 1881 Prince George, later King George V, was serving on HMS *Inconstant* in the Pacific Ocean. On a clear night he

Right *Nineteenth-century sailors sight the terrifying phantom known as the* Flying Dutchman.

and twleve other men saw a large old sailing ship drift just 200 metres off their bows. The strange ship was ablaze with a red light that seemed to glow from every part of her hull and masts. After being in view for some time the ship vanished as if the light had suddenly been switched off.

The *Flying Dutchman* is by no means the only phantom ship to sail the seas. On Christmas Day in 1752 the *Palatine* ran aground off Block Island, near the US state of Rhode Island. Local fishermen rescued the people on board the ship, but accidentally set fire to the ship in doing so. As the blazing wreck drifted out to sea, a woman was spotted on board. She screamed for help, but nobody could reach her in time. Many people have reported seeing the ghost of the blazing ship over the years. Equally tragic is the ghost of the *Lady Lovibund* which was wrecked on the Goodwin Sands in the English Channel, in 1748. It has been seen on the sands several times since.

Above *The treacherous Goodwin Sands at low tide with the shadow of the* Helena Modjeska *which ran aground and was wrecked earlier this century. It is here that the phantom ship the* Lady Lovibund *is said to be seen.*

Ghostly trains have also been 'seen' from time to time. A ghost train is reported to have appeared regularly on the Central Railway in Albany, New York. It was witnessed appearing each year on 27 April, for several years, starting in 1866. Almost everyone recognized the train. It was the spitting image of the funeral train of assassinated President Lincoln, which had passed through on its way from Washington to Illinois. For years afterwards, railway workers gathered at the side of the tracks on the evening of 27 April to watch the sad phantom train pass through.

Above *A lane in Leicestershire, near the site of the Battle of Bosworth (1485) which is said to be haunted by galloping horsemen.*

Left *Trick photography recreates the frightening spectacle of the phantom Number 7 bus which appeared in London several times in the 1930s.*

The ghostly accident

One of the most common types of ghost seen on the roads is that of a person who steps out in front of a vehicle. The driver often thinks he has hit somebody and stops, only to find nobody within sight. One such ghost haunts a main road (the A38) near Bristol, England. Several people have seen a woman leap in front of their cars on this road. A ghostly man in a strange hat behaves in the same way at West Hendred in Berkshire.

The most perplexing phantom of the road is the ghostly bus which once featured in a British court case. Late one night in 1936 a car crashed in St Mark's Road in Kensington, London, and the driver was killed. At the coroner's court the only witness to the accident was asked to state what he saw. Reluctantly the man stated that the driver had 'swerved to avoid the phantom number 7 bus'.

Though the coroner did not really believe this tale of a ghost bus, dozens of people wrote in to say that they had also seen the bus on other occasions. It was usually reported as speeding along St Mark's Road after dark. All the interior lights of the phantom were said to be switched on, but neither passengers nor driver could be seen. One employee of the bus company even said he had seen the bus arrive at the depot and then vanish. After alterations were made to St Mark's Road, the bus stopped haunting the area.

Even more up to date than ghostly buses and cars are the aeroplanes that have been reported haunting the skies. In recent years several people have seen a wartime Wellington bomber flying low along the Tywi valley in central Wales. Squadrons flying Wellingtons trained in this area during the Second World War, but no such plane has flown for many years.

The strange nature of the phantom machines has prompted some investigators to suggest a novel origin for these ghosts. Since machines cannot have souls or emotions it is said that witnesses might be looking through some kind of window in time. The ghost, the theory says, is a real object but is seen in two times at once. This argument can be followed to explain the appearances of several other types of ghost, particularly the phantom re-enactments of events. However, if this were the case we might expect people to see into the future. The crew of the Wellington bomber should have seen houses and buildings constructed since the war. No crews of Wellington bombers, or any other plane that flew during the Second World War, made such a report.

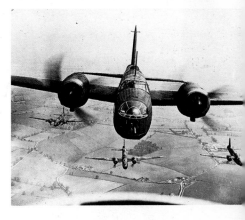

Above *Wellington bombers photographed during a wartime mission. In recent years 'ghosts' of these aircraft have been seen flying in Wales.*

A house possessed

It is 2.30 am on a July morning in 1951. A London policeman is dozing lightly in a house in Norwood, near London. The Greenfield family, who live in the house, have reported strange happenings. It seems that their house has been invaded by angry ghosts. The policeman is on guard in case a human intruder is to blame.

Suddenly a banging noise awakens the policeman. The sound is repeated. The policeman picks up his torch. He traces the noises to the bedroom of the family's ten-year-old daughter and throws open the door. What he sees makes him gasp in shock.

The girl is cowering against the far wall. In front of her a cardboard box is floating near the ceiling. A heavy wardrobe is rocking back and forth with loud bangs. Drawers drift out of a chest of drawers and hurtle across the room. For a few seconds the frightening performance continues. Then the policeman switches on the light. Immediately all the flying objects tumble to the ground and the cupboard becomes still. The policeman inspects all the objects for strings or other signs of trickery. They are perfectly normal. There is no explanation for what he has seen.

Houses of terror

Some ghosts seem to attach themselves to a particular house. They turn it into a place of terror, often forcing the people who live there to leave.

The unknown force which attacked the Greenfield family is fairly typical of a phenomenon labelled 'poltergeist', which is German for 'noisy ghost'. The activity began quietly with sounds like footsteps on the landing. After a few weeks small objects began to fly around the house when nobody could possibly have thrown them. For some reason vegetables seemed particularly likely to take to the air. After about three months heavy furniture and other objects were moving on their own. Eventually the family fled to stay with friends and sold the house. The trouble ceased immediately.

Poltergeists have been reported for hundreds of years. Their spectacular and often violent activities have made them favourite subjects for investigation. One of the earliest to be properly recorded was known as the Demon Drummer of Tedworth. The trouble began in March 1661 when a magistrate named Mompesson confiscated a drum belonging to a local beggar. The drum was placed in Mompesson's house at Tedworth. Soon afterwards strange bangs and hammerings were heard in the house.

After about a month the poltergeist seems to have discovered the drum. Night after night, for two months, the drum played itself for hours at a time. Then the haunting took a new turn. Mompesson's children were thrown out of bed several times, and floor boards ripped up. Shoes, books and clothes were thrown around the house by some invisible force. At one time the beggar claimed that he had caused the drum to play and the other disturbances himself, as revenge for Mompesson confiscating his drum. However, this claim was never proved; the true cause remains a mystery.

Above *A contemporary illustration depicting the Drummer of Tedworth as a devil. In fact the drummer was only seen once, and the witness was too frightened to give an accurate description.*

The Old City Hall of Toronto, Canada, is notorious for being haunted. Mysterious voices and footsteps have been heard and the temperature sometimes drops suddenly. A janitor working in the building said he was once 'rooted to the floor' by an invisible force. He was going down the back staircase when he felt something grip his ankles. The lights were on at the time, but there was nothing and no one around that could have held him down. One of the judges who presides in the courts there said, ' When I take the private judges' staircase, this thing catches my gown or gives me a gentle push every once in a while.' However, to this day, none of the strange happenings at the Old City Hall have been explained.

For centuries it was assumed that outbreaks of poltergeist activity were caused by a mischievous or evil spirit. The very name poltergeist indicates this belief. It was thought that some spirit had a grudge against the inflicted family and was taking revenge. Working on this belief some families have called in priests to conduct an exorcism. This involves casting out a demon spirit from a place or person.

Above *The Runcorn Poltergeist, suffered by the Glynn family in 1952, was fond of moving furniture about, and even when police kept watch the disturbances continued. John Glynn is seen in his wrecked bedroom in Cheshire, England.*

Sometimes an exorcism can calm or remove a poltergeist, but it is not always successful. In 1967 an American priest had just completed an exorcism when the poltergeist tipped a basket of dirty laundry over him.

Modern researchers, however, have come to a different conclusion about poltergeists. They believe that the phenomenon is caused by humans, though they have no control over what happens. Most poltergeist hauntings are centred on a single person, usually a teenager. Strange events only occur when that person is present, and sometimes follow them to different houses. Often these 'focus persons' are young and usually worried or anxious about something.

Investigators have suggested that the emotional power of these focus persons is translated into physical power. This power is able to move objects without the person actually touching them. It has even been credited with making objects appear from nowhere, a phenomenon known as an apport. This theory has become increasingly popular in recent years, however, the true cause of poltergeist activity remains a mystery.

Below *Some poltergeists seem to have a sense of humour. In the USA in 1967 one poltergeist threw a basket of dirty laundry at a priest who was trying to rid the house of its unwelcome guest.*

One of the most famous modern cases of a house being 'possessed' is that of the 'Amityville Horror' in the USA. In the winter of 1976, the owners of a house in the town of Amityville, in Long Island, New York, reported more than eighty incidents in the space of twenty-eight days.

George and Kathleen Lutz and their three children had only just moved into the house when they started hearing strange noises. Then they found windows and doors that they had locked to have been mysteriously forced open and for no apparent reason. They reported finding tracks like those of an enormous pig in the snow leading up to and away from the house. One night George Lutz woke up in bed to find his wife floating in the air above his bed. When he pulled her back down and put the light on, the woman who had seconds before been young and good-looking, suddenly appeared old and ugly. The couple said it was six hours before she returned to normal.

The Lutz family soon moved out of the house, and it was later discovered that the previous occupier, Ronald DeFeo, had murdered his family there. However, many people have since cast doubt on the truth of what the Lutz family claimed. Since the Lutz family left the house, there has been no repetition of the 'haunting' they say that they experienced.

Above *A scene from the movie* Poltergeist. *Like other types of ghost, poltergeists are a popular subject with the movie industry.*

Below *A terrifying incident from the movie* The Exorcist – *the priests attempt to cast a 'demon' from the girl.*

A dying man's ghost

It is February 1926 and the weather is calm over Killegar, County Leitrim, in Ireland. Miss Godley and her steward have just visited Robert Bowes, a retired man who used to work on her farm. He is lying ill in bed and has asked Miss Godley to call the doctor. Promising to do so, the visitors turn for home; their path takes them past a lake.

As they skirt the lake the travellers pause for a moment. The steward turns to Miss Godley and asks 'Can you see a man on the lake?' Miss Godley looks across the water and gasps in surprise. Poling a punt across the water is Robert Bowes, who they have recently left bedridden. Bowes takes no notice of Miss Godley. He continues across the lake to a bed of reeds and vanishes from sight. Miss Godley resumes her journey home.

When she returns home, Miss Godley sits down to write a message to the doctor asking him to visit Robert Bowes. Before the letter can be sent, news is received that Bowes is dead. He died in his bed at almost the same moment that Miss Godley and her steward saw him on the lake.

At the moment of death

Above *During the 1890s several photographers made a living by producing 'ghost' pictures like this one. Often photographers claimed that the images showed spirits returning from the grave. More rarely they said they were of 'crisis apparitions.'*

There is a kind of ghost that appears only once, hundreds of which have been seen by respectable witnesses. They are the ghosts that occur at the moment when a person dies. Sometimes the spectre is seen by someone who is very close to the dying person. On other occasions the ghost seems to wander to a place which it particularly liked when alive.

Though these ghosts seem to be rather common it is very difficult for researchers to investigate them. From their nature these phantoms only appear once. All researchers can do is talk to witnesses and collect information.

From such work it appears that these 'crisis apparitions' have several features in common. They appear to be completely solid and real to the witness. Though the apparitions can walk and move, they seem unable to speak. It also seems that the crisis apparitions usually appear at the actual moment of death. But on some occasions the spirit is seen several hours, or even days later.

It has been suggested that the human mind is capable of projecting an image over vast distances to appear to loved ones or in certain places. Only moments of extreme danger seem able to trigger this ability, hence the term 'crisis apparition'.

A typical example occurred in the spring of 1890. A young woman was working as a maid in a large house many kilometres from her family home in Grimsby. Early one morning, as she was crossing the hall, the maid saw her father. He was standing in the room dressed in his oilskins and dripping with water. As the startled girl was about to ask her father what he was doing so far from home, the father vanished. The girl collapsed in tears, convinced that something terrible had happened.

A few days later, news arrived that her father, a fisherman, had been drowned at sea.

Such phantoms do not appear only to relatives and loved ones. The ghost of Robert Bowes (see page 32) seems to have been roaming the countryside he loved so much. Rather more famous was the phantom admiral who visited his home in 1893. On 22 June 1893 Lady Tryon was holding a party for some friends in her house in Belgravia, London. Some of the guests were surprised to see Admiral Sir George Tryon walk into the room and then leave. He was supposed to be on his ship HMS *Victoria* in the Mediterranean at the time.

In fact the admiral was already dead, having drowned when his ship sank off the Syrian coast. For some reason Admiral Tryon had given orders which put the *Victoria* on collision course with HMS *Camperdown*. The captain of the *Camperdown* watched with amazement. He assumed that Tryon had some special plan in mind.

Above A sixteenth-century engraving showing the dripping ghost of a sailor appearing to his wife at the moment that his ship sank in a storm.

Left *The French magazine* Le Petit Jounal *of July 1893 depicts the fatal collision between the* Victora *and the* Camperdown *which resulted in the death of Admiral Tryon and 359 other men. Tryon's ghost is said to have appeared at his London home at this moment.*

By the time the astounded captain realized that his ship would collide with the *Victoria* it was too late. The two warships smashed together and the *Victoria* sank with the loss of 359 men.

The activities of these strange ghosts are not confined to people and places. It seems that a dying person can be concentrating on almost anything. Earlier this century, the framed certificate of qualification of a midwife in Liverpool fell off the wall of her house the very moment that she died.

The talking ghost

In 1888 an army officer was sleeping in barracks in Ireland when he awoke with a start. Standing by his bed appeared his elder brother who was serving in the army in South Africa. Thinking the figure really was his brother, the officer sat up and and said, 'Hello.'

'I am shot,' replied the figure.

'Shot?' exclaimed the man in bed, 'Where?'

'In the lungs,' replied the apparition, 'The general sent me forwards.' With these words he vanished. Only then did the man realize he had been speaking to a ghost. He later discovered that his brother had been killed that night by a bullet through the chest.

Further removed from the typical crisis apparition, seen at the moment of death, is the strange ghost of Ballachulish House, Scotland. For some years around the turn of the century Ballachulish was haunted by a phantom lady who roamed through the house at night. The ghost was very quiet and caused little trouble. Meanwhile, Lady Boulton, the wife of a well-known historian, was having a series of strange dreams. Each dream was the same. She found herself wandering through a house which she did not know. So often did Lady Boulton have this dream that she came to know the 'dream house' very well.

One day Sir Harold and Lady Boulton visited Ballachulish House to research some historical event. As they approached the house, Lady Boulton realized that it was her dream house. She was able to lead her husband through the rooms although she had never been there before. At the same time the staff at Ballachulish recognized Lady Boulton as their mysterious ghost. It seems that Lady Boulton had been somehow projecting her image to Ballachulish.

Below *The dramatic mountain scenery at Ballachulish. The historic Ballachulish House was troubled by a strange apparition.*

Bath's man in black

The year is 1986, Mrs Montefiore is walking along Saville Row towards the shops in Bath city centre in England. There are a few items that she wishes to buy. She runs through the list again to make sure that she has not forgotten anything. As she does so she notices a short, thin man walk around the corner in front of her.

She takes another look at the approaching man, as he is dressed rather strangely. He has a large black hat on his head and a wide cape around his shoulders. The cape is blown aside by the wind, revealing black breeches and stockings. Mrs Montefiore thinks this odd, but takes little more notice of the man.

As she comes within a few feet of the man in the black hat, Mrs Montefiore feels suddenly nervous, but does not know why. As she draws level with the man, he suddenly disappears. The startled woman steps backwards and stares around her. There are no doorways into which the man could have run. One second he was there, the next second he was gone.

Later Mrs Montefiore tells her friends about her frightening encounter. They tell her that the ghost in the black hat is often seen in that area of Bath.

Everyday ghosts

In this book we have looked at several different types of ghostly manifestations. We have seen that some ghosts re-enact dramatic events from the past, others appear for a specific purpose and a large number appear as crisis apparitions. However, the majority of ghostly sightings that people report fit into none of these categories.

Most incidents involving ghosts are rather ordinary and pointless. The ghost may appear only once, or be seen many times. Very often nobody even knows whose ghost it is.

Bath's man in black is typical of the quieter ghosts. It has been seen off and on for years, and is still being glimpsed. It seems quite content to stroll the streets appearing and vanishing quite suddenly. Nobody knows whose ghost it is, though from its dress it appears to date back about 300 years to the seventeenth century.

Equally disturbing is a phantom that has been reported near the village of Stanbridge in Hampshire. One evening in October 1979 a local man named Robert Fulton was driving along a lane when he spotted a hitch-hiker. The stranger was a young man in a white shirt. He did not say anything, but simply climbed into the car and sat quietly.

Right *Leiston churchyard, Suffolk, England. The graveyard is reputed to be haunted by a black dog. It is not known whether there is any connection with the Black Shuck (see page 16).*

Fulton accelerated up to about 60 kph and drove for a few minutes. He turned to ask the hitch-hiker where he would like to be dropped off, but the stranger had gone. The car door had not opened, yet the man had vanished. A similar phantom has been encountered in Somerset and a third in Kent. Vanishing hitch-hikers are not confined to Britain; many encounters have taken place in the USA. It seems that some ghosts delight in playing these tricks on mortals.

Such ghosts have been reported in many different places, but nowhere can boast more phantoms than the quiet Kent village of Pluckley. Several people out after dark have heard an invisible coach and horses trotting along the High Street. The churchyard is haunted by a woman in a red dress with a small white dog. A lane near the village is haunted by a long-dead schoolmaster and a phantom glow is seen on the spot where a woman was burnt to death.

Above *South African Dawie van Jaarsveld, who unwittingly gave a ride to a phantom woman hitch-hiker in April 1978. A woman had died in a road accident in the area.*

Left *A priest took this picture of his church at Newby, Yorkshire. When developed, it showed an ominous figure in black beside the altar.*

Returning to barracks

In the US Military Academy at West Point, New York, the apparition of a soldier is seen from time to time. The sightings always occur in one particular room of the 47th Division barracks. The apparition is of a soldier dressed in nineteenth century infantry uniform carrying his musket at his side. The ghost was investigated by a Captain Bakken, who saw the ghost for himself. He said the ghost, 'promptly appeared, but receded into the wall again, its point of exit [the place where it disappeared] was reported by the investigators to be icy to the touch'. Nothing else is known about the apparition, although some have claimed that it bears a resemblance to a soldier in a nineteenth century painting owned by the Academy.

A ghostly colonel wanders through nearby woods and a phantom monk paces a local farmyard.

Phantom monks seem particularly active at Beaulieu Abbey, now a stately home, in Hampshire. Dozens of people have seen ghost monks walking in the gardens. In 1965 one woman spotted a monk reading from a parchment. When she approached to see what was written, the figure vanished. So common are these sightings that the staff no longer take any notice of reports. Rather rarer is the sound of phantom singing. This has sometimes been heard and is generally described as tranquil and beautiful.

Nor are all ghosts exactly what they might seem to be. During the 1920s a strange apparition frightened several people who walked beside a pond in Brentford, near London, late at night. The witnesses reported seeing a large white object which rushed towards them out of the night. After several such reports the 'ghost' was revealed for what it was. One man was terrified by the pale phantom tearing towards him with a rushing noise. He dived for cover, but glanced up to see a swan flying by. It seems that the darkness and imagination had made the earlier witnesses think that they were being attacked by a ghost.

Above *The ruined Chapter House at Beaulieu Abbey, Hampshire, where the singing of phantom monks has been heard on numerous occasions.*

Perhaps one of the friendliest 'everyday ghosts' that people have claimed to have seen is that of the 'Good Ghost Sister' at the Prince Alfred Hospital in Sydney, Australia. This ghost is often mistaken by nurses and doctors for a real sister, and they only realize that 'she' is a ghost because 'she' vanishes into thin air.

On one occasion the ghost seems to have helped one of the nurses to spot a patient in trouble. Sister Bull said one night, 'I was working in one section of the ward when I saw what I thought to be the night sister bending over a patient in another part of the ward. I finished what I was doing and went over to see what the sister had discovered, but she disappeared while I was on the way. When I got to the patient I found that immediate attention was necessary.' It was then discovered that the night sister had not been in the ward at all – it seems it was the Good Ghost Sister.

Some people feel that the Good Ghost Sister is the ghost of a real sister, once on the staff, who died tragically as a result of a fall from a high balcony. If the sightings of the ghosts can be believed, it would seem that the ghost of the sister came back to carry on practising as a nurse in the hospital.

Conclusion

Above *Two photographs which seem to show a ghost materializing at a seance. Several investigators believe these pictures to be faked.*

So do ghosts exist? Hundreds of people have reported seeing ghosts. Some of these witnesses may have told their stories in order to gain attention. Perhaps they liked seeing their names in the newspapers and were willing to tell a false story in order to achieve this.

There are several instances where a supposed ghost has been explained away as something quite natural. For instance, around the turn of the century a house remained empty for some time due to the strange banging, swooshing and thumping noises that sounded from time to time. Eventually the house was leased out to a family for a very low rent. The family discovered that the sounds came from a drain connected to the house of a blacksmith shop about a kilometre away. The noises were echoes of activity in the shop. The 'haunting' was not due to a ghost at all.

There is no doubt that many reports of ghostly activity could be explained in some perfectly rational way. Some 'ghosts' are simply imagined by people. It is a well known fact that people who are worried about a subject may dream in such a way as to relieve their worries.

It has also been proved that these dreams may take the form of hallucinations seen when a person is awake. People who do not believe in ghosts explain most sightings away in terms of hallucinations. They say that 'ghosts' are created by the mind of the person who sees them.

Most experienced researchers, however, believe that a witness really does see a ghost. Several theories have been put forward to explain these sightings. It has been suggested that strong emotions may leave a psychic energy behind them. These may become visible in the form of a ghost.

Perhaps the wisest attitude to adopt is that of the US president of the 1930s and 1940s, Franklin Delano Roosevelt, who once told his wife: 'I think it is unwise to say you do not believe in anything when you can't prove that it is either true or untrue. There is so much in the world which is always new in the way of discoveries that it is wiser to say that there may be spiritual things which we are simply unable to fathom.'

Below *A time exposure photograph taken of Limassol Bay in Cyprus, in October 1986. When it was developed, the photograph showed a strange ghostly figure.*

Glossary

Apparition   Something that appears in an unusual way. A ghost is a form of apparition.

Apport   An appearance of an object, apparently out of nothing.

Breeches   Old-fashioned trousers that reach down only to the knee.

Cavaliers   Supporters of King Charles I during the English Civil War.

Civil war   A war fought between groups of people from the same country.

Coroner's court   A court of law held to determine the cause of a sudden or unexplained death of a person.

Corpse   A dead body, especially of a person.

East Indies   An old name for Indonesia.

Exorcise   To free something or someone from evil spirits by prayers or by a religious ceremony.

Free French   Those French soldiers who continued to fight against Germany during the Second World War after France had surrendered.

Hallucination   A type of waking dream in which a person 'sees' an object or person which is not actually present.

Haunted   A word describing a place that is frequently visited by a ghost or ghosts.

Landing craft   A kind of ship used in war to put soldiers and weapons ashore.

Monk   A man who is a member of a religious group that lives a life of religious devotion away from the rest of the world.

Psychic energy   A force which some people think is released by people when they experience strong emotions.

Punt   A flat-bottomed boat which is moved by means of pushing on a long pole against the bottom of the river or lake.

Re-enactment   The replaying of a scene or situation.

Roundheads   The supporters of Parliament during the English Civil War.

Scaffold   A wooden platform on which people were executed.

Supernatural   Something that it is not possible to explain in terms of the laws of nature – as yet ghosts are supernatural.

Telepathy   The alleged ability of two people to communicate with each other by brain power alone.

Wellington   A type of two-engined British bomber used during the Second World War.

Winkle   A small type of edible shellfish with a spiralled shell.

Further reading

If you would like to discover more about some of the ghosts and strange encounters mentioned in this book and others, you may like to read the following books:

Alexander, Marc, *Haunted Houses You May Visit* (Sphere Books, 1982)

Blundell, Nigel, and Boar, Roger *The World's Greatest Ghosts* (Octopus, 1983)

Hippisley Coxe, Antony, *Haunted Britain* (Hutchinson, 1973)

Knight, David, *Poltergeists: Hauntings and Haunted* (J.M. Dent, 1977)

Matthews, Rupert, *The Spinechilling Book of Horror* (Hamlyn, 1988)

Matthews, Rupert, *The Supernatural* (Wayland, 1989)

Picture Acknowledgements

The publishers would like to thank the following for supplying pictures for use in this book: Aldus Archive 17, 18 (top); Janet and Colin Bord 24 (top), 40; David Bowden Photographic Library 18 (bottom), 43 (bottom); Bruce Coleman 43 (top); Mary Evans Picture Library 10 (bottom), 11, 13 (top), 22 (bottom), 36; Fortean Picture Library 6 (bottom), 7, 12, 19 (bottom), 22 (top), 28, 29, 35, 41 (top and bottom), 45; The Kobal Collection 6 (top); National Film Archive 31 (top and bottom); Topham Picture Library 13 (bottom), 23, 24 (bottom), 25, 34, 37, 42, 44; Zefa Picture Library 10 (top), 19 (top).

Index

B17104

DATE DUE

-9.OCT.1989	8.MAR.1991	24. OCT 2005
		15. JUN. 2006
24.NOV.1989 BM	22.JUL.1991	
-6.APR.1990	20.SEP.1991	31. MAY 2007
-6.APR.1990	?.	
12.APR.1990	20.MAR.1992 -2.APR.1993	
12.APR.1990	1 8 APR 1994	
-1.JUN.1990	2 5 NOV 1994	
-8.JUN.1990		
Sue Delaney 17.AUG.1990	2 - MAR 1995 -1 MAR 1996	
22.FEB.1991	1 5 JUN 1996	
-3.MAR.1991		
-8.MAR.1991	2 7 APR 1998	RAECO